YOUR KNOWLEDGE HAS VALUE

- We will publish your bachelor's and master's thesis, essays and papers

- Your own eBook and book - sold worldwide in all relevant shops

- Earn money with each sale

Upload your text at www.GRIN.com and publish for free

Gebhard Deißler

Cultural identity. Interdependence of Diversity

GRIN Publishing

Bibliographic information published by the German National Library:

The German National Library lists this publication in the National Bibliography; detailed bibliographic data are available on the Internet at http://dnb.dnb.de .

Imprint:

Copyright © 2013 GRIN Verlag GmbH
Print and binding: Books on Demand GmbH, Norderstedt Germany
ISBN: 978-3-656-56692-2

This book at GRIN:

http://www.grin.com/en/e-book/214557/cultural-identity-interdependence-of-diversity

GRIN - Your knowledge has value

Since its foundation in 1998, GRIN has specialized in publishing academic texts by students, college teachers and other academics as e-book and printed book. The website www.grin.com is an ideal platform for presenting term papers, final papers, scientific essays, dissertations and specialist books.

Visit us on the internet:

http://www.grin.com/

http://www.facebook.com/grincom

http://www.twitter.com/grin_com

Transcultural Management

Gebhard Deißler D.E.A./UNIV. PARIS I

THE ONLY WAY

CULTURE   RESEARCH

KULTUR FORSCHUNG

RECHERCHE CULTURE

BÚSQUEDA CULTURAL

RICERCA   CULTURALE

跨文化的智慧精髓

Итранскультурная

Interkulturelles- u. Transkulturelles Management (German)

Intercultural &Transcultural Management (English)

Gestion Interculturelle et Gestion Transculturelle (French)

Gerencia Intercultural y Gerencia Transcultural (Spanish)

Gerência Intercultural e Gerência Transcultural (Portuguese)

跨文化的智慧精髓 - kua wen hua de zhi hui jing sui (Chinese)

транскультурная компетенция - transkulturnaja
kompetencija (Russian)

toransukaruchā　・ manējimento (Japanese)
トランスカルチャー　・　マネジメント

THE ONLY WAY

Identifying one's own way means acknowledging the other, for it defines itself only through and by the other. It consecrates interdependence and points to a superordinate unity, based on the interdependence of diversities in a vaster organism of mankind – provided that interdependence is understood and respected. Conversely, thoughtless, though maybe well-meaning rejection of one's own way negates the entire field with its interdependence-based unity. Therefore the repression or oblivion of one's way or cultural identity necessarily fires back at the diverse socio-cultural entities of the human organism as a whole and thereby impedes human unity and integration as a path to global peace.

It is important to appreciate the interconnectedness of the world we are living in at socio-cultural level and the interdependence of the parts with the whole as well as the parts among each other as well as the fact that it starts with the acknowledgement of one's own way in the respect of the interdependent other way rather than at its expense, which has been the case for ages. And that was and is the cause of socio-cultural conflict, with its political and economic ramifications.

In today's global world a new understanding of alterity is required that is inclusive rather than exclusive in one's own as well as everybody else's interest who are all part of the human social organism. As anything this may by abused by those who interpret it in a selfish way by implicitly saying to other interdependent parts of the social organism: "You shoulder my responsibility, while I sleep and let you do my work." This is a lack of social responsibility based on a misunderstanding of one's way and related responsibility with regard to the interdependent ways. It results in an overburdening of the interdependent organs of the social organism by the part of the organism that misunderstands or misconstrues interdependence-based unity and structural and functional integrity of the organism as a whole. Physiologically it corresponds to as state of disease, where an organ does not perform its healthy functions. But, as a rule, this state is not induced by human idiosyncrasy and indifference or lack of understanding of social co-responsibility of the parts among each other and the parts and the whole but it is part of the biography and the mindset of that part. It will and must therefore be taken care of by interdependence-based solidarity of the parts and the whole.

This metaphorical physiological conception of social organisms can be used for many types of social analysis, particularly, if more players are involved, as is the case in today's increasingly complex and multidimensional world. Actually it is not new, but humans tend to forget or ignore it due to individual and social self-interest and therefore construe interdependence antagonistically as what can be termed a win-lose or zero-sum game that affects everybody adversely in the longer term. Then the part that indulges in such behaviour expands viciously like as social cancer that devours the parts of the organism and leads to its destruction. This may occur at the political, economic, ideological and cultural level in a similar way as it does at the organic level. The principles of life follow similar patterns in the diverse contexts where life manifests itself.

It can also be understood from a systems analysis standpoint which has become popular with the growing need of management in an increasingly complex scientific and technical world. But today the complexity of the material world tends to be paralleled by the complexity of the socio-cultural world due to demographic changes and multiculuralization and the pluralism that goes with them. This state of affairs needs a corresponding change towards an interdependence-based ethics in the interest of the interdependent parts of the social organism as a whole, for any voluntary or involuntary dysfunctionality of a part is bound to affect the organism as a whole as well as its myriad parts. The assumption that some part may be victimized by others for their own advantage at the detriment of the former without impacting interdependent parts and last but not least the part that holds this erroneous assumption and behaves accordingly is inappropriate as it will turn out to backfire on the parts that would like to take advantage of interdependence. It is merely a matter of time when the pendulum swings back for it cannot remain in a state of lopsidedness and imbalance. Therefore political, economic and socio-cultural imbalances are reversed in the longer-term based on the need of balance inherent in systems. Otherwise they may perish as a whole. And in order to prevent the end of a system as a whole its internal dynamics of interdependence-based equilibrium need to be restored.

Physiological disease, political uprising or sociocultural unrest and economic crises may be seen as processes of life preserving self-regulation of systems based on all-pervasive biological principles of life in its myriad forms and manifestations. The biological cycles in man and nature and their interconnected environments may illustrate aspects of that principle and if it is interfered with the ecosystems and their inhabitants suffer accordingly as well. Wherever the eyes of the observer of that nature of life and its manifestations may turn, the principle pointed to works in order to allow the expression of life in its own way, in life's way, for which there is neither ersatz, nor even improvement – for it is whole and requires neither addition nor subtraction and only its unhampered unfolding – but only deoptimization through undue human interference.

What is required is an understanding of the specific expression of life per se or the way of life in a specific manifestation of that principle of life. Depending to the place a part occupies in an organism as a whole the unfathomable wisdom of life correspondingly enables different structures and functions. This principle has created structural-functional diversity that maintains interdependence-based unity of organisms. Anatomy and physiology of the human physical organism unveil structural functional diversity of the diverse part that make up man as a whole. And when every part expresses the one principle of life in its functionally required way with regard to the whole homeostasis and harmony prevail that are hallmarks of life and its proper flow and manifestation or expression.

This may again be translated to other levels of existence such as the socio-cultural, where life needs to manifest its timeless, unchangeable way in a similar way. Life per se will have to express itself in individually and culturally specific ways so as to viabalize interdependency-based social organisms. Ignoring functionally specific expression of life in nature or man means negating interdependence and therefore interdependence-based wholeness and thereby nature and mankind in their diversity as we know it.

A personal ethic and accountability of the part with regard to the whole, of the individual towards society or of the culture with regard to humanity may be inferred form that understanding. Such is the assumption of more Western, individualistic cultures, whereas in more Eastern, collectivistic cultures, where the individual is construed as interdependent with its in-group may therefore tend to a group-based ethic and accountability and ask what the group owes the individual based on the individuals compliance with group norms. Whatever the culturally diverse prioritization within the manifestation of life as a whole may be, that prioritization leads to the complementary parts of the whole and has to ensure that it accounts for interdependent parts of the whole for its own sake as well as in the interest of the whole on which all its parts are contingent and vice versa. Depending on the side of the coin that is culturally viewed first an individual or group-based ethics have evolved to viabalize the expression of the principle of life.

However, with the relativization of individual or group ethics the expression of life is impaired in the diverse human spheres of life, the cultural, the economic or the political and at its diverse scales, locally, regionally, nationally and internationally. Thus ethics as the norms that enable interdependence-based harmonious expression of life is a requirement of life and its healthy manifestation and it becomes increasingly important with the growing number of interdependent parts of social wholes. And the explanation for malfunctioning social wholes in world economy, politics and culture consists in the loss of the parallelization of the number of the parts of wholes and the ethical accountability of those increased players. The globalization-specific challenge of our time therefore consists in a reparallelization of ethics as the code of conduct for the unhampered manifestation of interdependence-based living social wholes with the growing number of players and parts of globally expanding wholes.

The understanding of live as interdependence-based unity has fallen into oblivion through secularization. Ethical relativization that came with has undermined the survival of many living systems, including man himself as well as his artifacts and keeps on doing so. Man prioritized material expressions of life and lost the enigma of life as a whole out of sight. Life as a whole slipped in a dead angle. And as long as its interdependence-based logic along with its enabling ethic are not viewed as inseparably complementary aspects, mental, social and material dysfunctionalities will continue, for the principle is one, while the forms are many.

The foundation for this understanding has in particular been laid by Christian Civilization and the key and panacea for the perfect expression of life has been formulated as the twofold commandment of love that enables the law of life in the best possible way as it entails perfect interdependence for the sake of the whole and all its pars. Yet, with secularization the source and the foundation of true life and the understanding of its interdependence-based expression progressively waned from the horizon of human awareness and thereby the very source of life as well as the understanding of its nature. If this human condition was irreversible, mankind would be doomed, for it has tried to evolve independently of the source of life and its true understanding from the source with its interdependence-based flow in creation as well as, in particular, without the due consideration of the author that created this life and therefore its manifestations. We can trace them back, identify life's interdependency-based principle as well as its primal source and thus rejuvenate life and its expressions from the very source if we desecualrize life and recover its mystic unity within the Creator. What is needed is the complementary view to the manifestation of life, which is its source, and the integration of both expressed in its interdependency-based principle. When the whole reappears in man's perception, along with its code of expression, life can unfold anew in its in man's perception way, the only way! The way of life, the only way of interdependence-based unity from its source and with its code communication is aptly epitomized in many parables of the Christian Bible. One of them, namely that of the Vine and the Branches can be found on the concluding pages of this exposé.

As the foundation of life, society, cultures and civilizations across time and space it has been consecrated by Christianity and in particular by Jesus Christ, the Founder and living incarnation of that true understanding of life, 2000 years ago. The Trinity itself appears as interdependency in unity of Father, Son and Holy Spirit that in turn are inseparably interdependent with man and Creation. This archetypal interdependency-based unity is reflected at all levels of creation. The compliance with it brings with it an interdependency-based ethics of co-responsibility and solidarity that enables live, whereas its absence impedes it. Therefore, understanding any manifestation of life, social, cultural, political, scientific etc. requires the understanding of life per se.

Any social, political, cultural, ecological and other human problems can be solved on the basis of an understanding of the archetypal principle of interdependency-based unity that underpins and permeates the world. Anything outside this law of creation is its negation. It introduces an antagonism that corrupts unity of life and its integrity at the source and cannot pretend to be part of the Creator's Creation but is its antithesis and needs to be rejected for the sake of truth and life as the Only Way, which is the way of light and life as opposed to the way of darkness and death. It is the way of love and justice in God as opposed to the way of hate and antagonism, between individuals and cultures. The latter are neither an expression nor a manifestation of life from its source but a corrupting perversion of life that ends it at whatever level of existence. These two antagonistic forces have been identified by the Creator of all life as God and the devil, the spirit that negates all life in order to establish his reign of darkness and death. And the entire Creation is caught in this struggle between the true light of God and the darkness of what is not God, of what does not come from Him.

These two faces of the world need to be understood and the right side has to be chosen. This ultimate eschatological transcendent-immanent interdependency-based unity also needs to be understood if man is to flourish as intended by his Creator. The antagonist darkens this understanding in order to deceive man into thinking that he is the ruler. But darkness is ultimately relative to light and the Source of Life and Light forever rules over the shadow of death. This is the meaning of resurrection, the victory over death and the triumph of light and life eternal. The human mind that is established in the resurrection enigma takes part in life and light eternal, which is the natural complement of terrestrial life and completes the unity of all life, by which all earthly problems can be solved. And the personified expression of this mystery is contained in a single word: Jesus Christ the Saviour - and his work of salvation and redemption of man and Creation that frees them from that what is their negation. Thus the mystically resurrected man in Christ is himself the only incarnated way that begins where others end.

Other ways correspond to different levels of maturity and insight or lead into the wrong direction. Ultimately they turn out to be false and therefore have to end.

When their light is fading and they offer no issue the redeeming way may lead the true seeker on the way to his true home, not the many provisional homes. Some pretend to be on the right way but seek to take advantage of fellow-travelers and are therefore bandits on the way – wolves in sheep's clothing. Due to the snares on the way one should consider no one truly fortunate before his end, as the scriptures advise us.

The lyrics of the well-known song Amazing Grace testify to the human intuition of the one way and its destination as well as to the perils of the journey and man's trust in the grace of the only one way that leads him home, to his true home; the Eternal Home of His Creator and Father:

> ...Through many dangers, toils and snares
> I have already come;
> 'Tis Grace that brought me safe thus far
> and Grace will lead me home...

The Vine and the Branches

15 "I am the true vine, and my Father is the gardener. [2] He cuts off every branch in me that bears no fruit, while every branch that does bear fruit he prunes[a] so that it will be even more fruitful. [3] You are already clean because of the word I have spoken to you. [4] Remain in me, as I also remain in you. No branch can bear fruit by itself; it must remain in the vine. Neither can you bear fruit unless you remain in me.

[5] "I am the vine; you are the branches. If you remain in me and I in you, you will bear much fruit; apart from me you can do nothing. [6] If you do not remain in me, you are like a branch that is thrown away and withers; such branches are picked up, thrown into the fire and burned. [7] If you remain in me and my words remain in you, ask whatever you wish, and it will be done for you. [8] This is to my Father's glory, that you bear much fruit, showing yourselves to be my disciples.

[9] "As the Father has loved me, so have I loved you. Now remain in my love. [10] If you keep my commands, you will remain in my love, just as I have kept my Father's commands and remain in his love. [11] I have told you this so that my joy may be in you and that your joy may be complete. [12] My command is this: Love each other as I have loved you. [13] Greater love has no one than this: to lay down one's life for one's friends. [14] You are my friends if you do what I command. [15] I no longer call you servants, because a servant does not know his master's business. Instead, I have called you friends, for everything that I learned from my Father I have made known to you. [16] You did not choose me, but I chose you and appointed you so that you might go and bear fruit—fruit that will last—and so that whatever you ask in my name the Father will give you. [17] This is my command: Love each other.

John 15

Source. BibleGateway.com